When Your Best Friend Becomes Your Old Friend

How to Care For Your Geriatric Canine

By: Gina Stewart
Don and Kellie Rainwater

Table of Contents

Chapter One: Why We Wrote This Book

Why I Wrote This Book – Gina Stewart

The reason why I wrote this book is twofold.

The first reason is to help understand the passing of a dearly beloved friend from childhood. Since it was many years ago for me but more recently for my mother and a few of my friends, I wanted to understand the grief that consumes them for such a long period of time and still hurts them when the mention of their dogs comes up in casual conversation.

When I lost the only dog I ever had when I was only 16 years old. My grief was pushed aside because I was busy with teenage stuff and I didn't know how to properly grieve.

The second reason I wrote this book is because my beloved dog Brownie, a German short-haired Pointer, turns six this year which means she is entering her senior years, especially for her breed. I hear a crackling sound when I wipe off her paws when she comes in from the rain. She's gained a little weight around her midsection, which we need to take care of as soon as possible because weight around the midsection in an older dog spells trouble, and if we can remove it she will live longer.

You want your dog to live forever because she is your constant companion, your best friend, your confidant and someone who doesn't judge you for what you do or say and that is truly a best friend.

Why We Wrote This Book – Don and Kellie Rainwater

My wife and I helped write this book because our 14 year old Labrador retriever was on his last legs. My four-legged son Rock had been with me several years before I met my wife Kellie. Both Rock and I spent 10 wonderful years with his new mommy and my new wife. Toward the end of his life Rock began to hobble because of arthritis and other ligaments injuries, turn gray around his mouth and belly fur, and his eyes began to grow black with cataracts.

My wife and I did a lot of research to find out how to make his last years more pleasant. Though he needed help getting up and down the stairs, getting in the car, and even getting up to go outside, he still tried to please his master by hiding the pain he was in. He would still lay his head in my lap so I could pet his long floppy ears. He would look at me but couldn't see me. He would wag his tail, not because he wanted to, but he knew it would make me feel more comfortable. When my wife was sick, he would lay his head on the bed at her side and comfort her.

He was my best friend and now he was my old friend, and I had to make his life more comfortable. Kellie and I searched the internet, read tons of books, and learned all we could about how to take care of geriatric dogs. With the help of the co-author Gina Stewart, I think we have compiled a helpful guide to help your old friend through their senior years and across the rainbow bridge when it is time to say goodbye.

Some of this book is as hard to write as you the reader will find it is sometimes hard to read. If tears could have damaged our keyboards as we wrote, Gina, Kellie, and I would have gone through many. As this book came together, Rock passed away on May 5th, 2008. He lived a full and happy life. He traveled across the country with us five times. He got to stay at the kennels at Disney World and even earned a certificate there for good behavior. He never yelped in pain or groaned in discomfort. He put himself before us and the other smaller dogs we have in our family.

As I write this, I hope he is waiting for me on the other side with a tennis ball in his mouth, a spring in his step, a wag in his tail, and ready to run through the tall grass and swim in the streams. I miss my boy.

Rainbow Bridge

Just this side of heaven is a place called Rainbow Bridge.
When an animal dies that has been especially close to someone here, that pet goes to Rainbow Bridge. There are meadows and hills for all of our special friends so they can run and play together. There is plenty of food, water, and sunshine, and our friends are warm and comfortable.

All the animals that had been ill and old are restored to health and vigor. Those who were hurt or maimed are made whole and strong again, just as we remember them in our dreams of days and times gone by. The animals are happy and content, except for one small thing; they each miss someone very special to them, who had to be left behind.

They all run and play together, but the day comes when one suddenly stops and looks into the distance. His bright eyes are intent. His eager body quivers. Suddenly he begins to run from the group, flying over the green grass, his legs carrying him faster and faster.

You have been spotted, and when you and your special friend finally meet, you cling together in joyous reunion, never to be parted again. The happy kisses rain upon your face; your hands again caress the beloved head, and you look once more into the trusting eyes of your pet, so long gone from your life but never absent from your heart.

Then you cross Rainbow Bridge together....

Author unknown...

Chapter Two: Your Older Dog's Diet Can Add Extra Time to Their Life

Changing Your Dog's Diet

Your dog seems to eat everything in sight and that doesn't hurt. Especially when he was young it seemed like his stomach was made of heavy metal. When you're going to change your pet's diet it is best to do it gradually and that means take at least four days to switch him over to the new food. If your dog is older, take special care in changing his diet. He may need a new diet because of aliments, but don't upset his stomach with sudden changes in his eating habits.

Since this change should be gradual, have plenty of the old food available the first day. Mix the food with three quarters old food and a quarter new. In two days you can add in another quarter of new food and do that again in two days until the food is all new. If you change your dog's diet suddenly he can get sick with these symptoms: stomach cramps, heartburn, indigestion, diarrhea, and vomiting. He may also refuse to eat at all.

Another thing you don't want to do is constantly switch your dog's food. Just because a dog food is on sale doesn't mean your dog's food needs changing. On the contrary, this will make your dog sick. Some experts say you should change your dog's food periodically, but not often. They say this helps prevent any dietary excesses or deficiencies from becoming a problem. But a very important reason may be to prevent allergies. Allergies build up over time with daily exposure. The cases of developing an allergy suddenly are rare.

The most frequent allergies are to foods that have been in dog foods for years. The advice from nutritionists is that a variety of foods from a young age will help prevent allergies. This is good news for your dog if you do this before he ages. Just as in humans, the older the dog is the more likely he is to have allergies. Time and the same food for years are enemies of your respiratory health in reference to allergies. There are common signs to alert you that your dog may have allergies.

These signs are itchy skin, red itchy paws, chewing paws, yeast infections, and ear infections. Also, skin infections that return after treatment with antibiotics have stopped. This means you need to change your dog's food periodically. That means that the main ingredient should differ from the previous food. It's pretty straightforward; if the main ingredient in his food has been beef, then switch to a main ingredient of chicken, lamb, or turkey. You may wonder if you need to change brands every time. No. But many of the ingredients should be different, especially the main one. Changing every three months is a good ratio.

Some people think changing dog foods periodically will make their dog picky. Well, no it won't. It will help him stay interested in his diet. Dogs get bored too. And some dog's stomachs don't get upset when you change the food, but to be sure that this allergy prevention method doesn't upset your dog's digestive tract, do it gradually each time as stated above.

Gastrointestinal Problems and Your Dog

Several different gastrointestinal diseases can arise to afflict your dog. These problems are digestion problems, diarrhea, nausea, loose stools, gas, irritable bowel, colitis, bloat-torsion, liver or kidney damage, and eating grass or feces. The intestinal track is made to digest and absorb nutrients. That's why nutrition is important in preventing and treating gastrointestinal disorders. Usually acute gastrointestinal problems are caused by poor diet. Vomiting and diarrhea are acute. Stopping food intake for twenty-four to forty-eight hours is a normal request from your vet. This will rest your dog's bowel and it will reduce the amount of unabsorbed nutrients in his bowel.

Sometimes water should be withheld too. This approach should help stop the vomiting and diarrhea. When these signs of the disease have stopped, you can give your pet some water. If he doesn't get sick from the water then you can give him some food. A bland diet is the usual one recommended in these cases. Basically, this is food that's low-fat and easy to digest. Cottage cheese and rice works well for dogs. If your dog eats this food, then a therapeutic diet for the treatment of gastrointestinal disease will be recommended. These are very digestible and contain moderate or low fat.

If your dog isn't vomiting, but he does have diarrhea, then your vet may treat him with an oral dehydration solution. The solutions contain carbohydrates, amino acids, and electrolytes like potassium and sodium. Only use products that are made for pets because the ones made for humans could harm your dog. He has different nutritional requirements than people do. The use of these solutions and semi-solid food could make the diarrhea worse before your pet gets better. If this occurs contact your vet for help. If the health issue isn't chronic then your vet will suggest that you feed your dog his regular diet after a few days to a week.

Dogs are known to eat grass and really its part of their ancestral habits as dogs are omnivores. Sometimes they eat grass because their stomach is upset and grass can induce them to vomit. But many times when a dog is feeling well and outside playing he will munch on some grass. Their stomachs are equipped with neuro-recepters and these react to what a dog eats. The neuro-recepters are sensitive to acidity, chemical content, and textures. In the wild they ate many herbivores and they ate the entire animal so that they ate the partially digested plants in the other animal's stomach.

Gas build up is an effect of gastrointestinal problems and your dog's stomach can become so gaseous that his stomach becomes bloated or distended. It will be hard when you touch it. Another problem is feeding your dog bones, this is a practice that we grow up believing to be good for our dogs, but it is a bad habit. Bones can cause different problems. The obvious is splintering, thus they sometimes stick in the colon or esophagus. When one is stuck in the esophagus it can prevent swallowing. These bones have to be removed by a vet.

How-to Help an Aging Dog Lose Weight

We've established that a dog can be overweight and this is more likely to happen as he ages. There is a twofold reason: He eats too much food or the wrong food and doesn't exercise enough. For your pet to lose weight it's necessary for you to want him to lose weight. Your grown dog doesn't need to be feed three or four times a day like when he was a puppy and he doesn't need a constant supply of food in his bowl.

Obesity isn't confined to the human population, but your dog needs you to lose weight. A pregnant or nursing dog needs more food, but we're not addressing that issue here. Some dog owners prepare special diets for their dogs from recipes that are healthier for their dogs. That's a good idea, but using table scraps to feed your dog isn't good for him. Those scraps will make him overweight, which can make him age faster and high calorie human foods are bad for your dog. Those table scraps are bad for your dog in other ways as some of the spices can be unhealthy for your pet.

There are special formulas dog foods that are made for aging dogs and these address losing weight among other health issues. One of the obvious issues is the health of your dog's heart. The best thing to do is to put your older dog on a geriatric or senior dog formula that will help keep him from becoming obese or help him lose weight and it will be more easily digested to help him get the most out of the nutrients.

Your dog uses fat as his basic energy source. A good low-calorie alternative is achieved by replacing some of the fat with highly digestible carbohydrates. Digestible carbohydrates have one half or less of the calories of fat in an equal amount. Indigestible fiber has disadvantages for your dog that digestible carbohydrates don't have. Your dog needs a diet with a normal fiber level and the fiber source should be moderately fermented. This helps to repair his gut and maintain a healthy gut. A healthy gut condition is vital in his weight reduction program.

Be sure that the weight loss formula you choose doesn't dilute the calories with high fiber levels. High fiber foods can lessen digestibility and absorption of numerous nutrients. This includes fats. This will cause your dog to lose weight at the expense of good nutrition. High fiber diets can also hurt the skin and coat condition. A diet that adjusts the fatty acid profile while lowering the fat level will maintain your dog's healthy coat and skin. When rice is the primary carbohydrate source in your dog's diet, his blood sugar levels may rise.

But corn, sorghum and barley may lower his blood sugar and insulin level, which can help your dog lose weight, also l-carnitine, which is an amino acid that helps burn fat. You should have a goal of helping your dog lose weight gradually. Dogs should lose one to two percent of their original weight each week. Being overweight can aggravate other health problems like arthritis.

Hunting Dogs and Nutrition

You just can't feed your hunting dog the way you did years ago because you'll be behind other hunting dog owners in field trials. If they follow more modern methods and you don't, you've let them have the edge over you. Amongst these newer methods is the use of antioxidants. All bird dog trainers nowadays are using or looking for that different diet or feeding method that will keep his dog on top so his head stays up and he hunts the length of the field trial. This better diet will be especially important for the older bird dog.

Carotenoid is an important antioxidant. Antioxidants have an effect on the immune system and that's significant for your hunting dog because he's a working dog. Carotenoids make the color in fruits and vegetables. Beta-carotene, lutein, and vitamins

A.,C. and E. stop massive tissue damage, which free radicals cause in their absence or when they are low in your dog's system. Free radicals roam your dog's body and damage or destroy healthy cells. This is called perioxidation.

Your bird dog hunts in conditions of cold and wet and he's under stress. Stress alone causes him to need more vitamins and particularly antioxidants. The production of free radicals rises under these conditions. Older field trial dogs are at greater risk. The research conducted for humans and by Iams and other dog food makers have proven that adult dogs and older dogs even more so need antioxidants to prevent disease. Research also indicates that all of the antioxidants are needed.

Your bird dog also needs energy to compete in field trials and that comes from calories and fat has advantages over carbohydrates. They should get about twenty percent of fat in their food to get the energy they need while under this stress. Dogs also get energy from protein and hunting dogs are no exception. Make sure he gets adequate protein in his diet. Overall make sure he gets a balanced diet. The beagle is a hunting dog that some owners think stays healthier on a diet of lamb and rice.

Hunting dogs need to be given a healthy diet so they don't become overweight because they have to be in good shape to hunt. Greyhounds need particular care with their diet because they'll become bloated if they eat large amounts of food at a time. They should be feed three small meals every day. Some owners of hunting dogs recommend the Pro Balanced Formula for the best nutrition for your hunting dog. They say that the high protein it contains give the extra energy a working dog has to have.

These working dogs definitely need special care and attention. Remember that they incur more injuries and need their immune system functioning as well as it can. Also, fat and protein will give them the energy they need. Your hunting dog is a friend and a fellow sportsman that depends on you for training, love, and his health needs and he will need your help more as he ages.

Older Dogs Intelligence and Diet

We've all heard that certain supplements may help reverse cognitive aging in humans, but it seems there is hope for an old dog that is losing cognitive function too and that supplements are the answer. Researchers from the Linus Pauling Institute at Oregon State University, the University of Toronto, University California/Berkeley, Children's Hospital Oakland Research Institute, and Juvenon, Inc. published a study in 2007 in the FASEB Journal. It was produced by the Federation of American Societies for Experimental Biology.

The research was with these two supplements: acetyl-l-carnitine and alpha lipoic acid. They are researching these nutrients ability to help with the repair of neurodegeneration and cognitive decline that's common in the aging process in humans. These researchers saw improvement in geriatric beagle dog's ability to learn new tricks that is to say tasks they hadn't done before. These two nutrients are antioxidants. They think that they help decrease mitochondrial decay in the cell.

In this study they taught inbred older beagles to find a treat. They had to learn to identify signs like a yellow wooden peg. The scientists used scent controls too so they couldn't use their sense of smell. In a task, four of six dogs that had been given the supplements found the food because they could identify the marker. Two dogs on the non-supplemented diet found the treat. (This information was adapted from Science Daily)

Dogs perceive their environment through cognitive ability, which is dependent on its degree of sensorial acuity. As a dog ages it needs more protection against free radicals attacking the brain, nervous system and other systems in its body. There are other antioxidants that help cognitive function like vitamin E and vitamin C because it helps vitamin E to regenerate. A breed like poodle's which have a greater longevity needs these antioxidants even more so and it seems that older dogs respond to training better if given antioxidants.

There are better commercial foods that have more antioxidants and you can get supplements for your dog. If you want to make your dogs food you can find recipes for this that include antioxidant rich foods. Though some people would disagree, if you have owned many dogs, you've probably noticed that he has some reasoning power. It's elemental but he has it. Guide dogs and hunting dogs handle situations where they have to size it up and make elemental decisions. Dogs have great scent memory capacity and good sound memory function.

You can tell he has this knack for remembering sounds because he'll remember a voice he hasn't heard in years. Dogs learn, but it's more memory than understanding the way we do. He has some ability to learn the cause and effect of his actions like in house training or catching a Frisbee. With your dog's intelligence to protect, you'll want to give him the best nutritional help you can to aid in his geriatric years and it's best to start when he is younger so his cells don't oxidize as much.

Some Breeds Age Slower Than Others

One of these signs of aging is when your dog isn't as frisky as before. Just as your body and mind changes as you age, so does your dog's body and mind change with aging. Still your dog can stay healthier and more active with the proper care. Different breeds age differently, meaning that some are older at six years and other later on. The average age at which dogs reach old age is seven years depending on their breed and size. Large does usually age faster than smaller dogs. None-the-less, there are certain signs of aging in all dogs that you can notice.

One thing that makes your dog less frisky as he ages is his metabolism slows down. Your dog's body metabolism reacts to aging in a similar manner to yours. It slows down when he ages and he begins to gain weight, particularly when he's eating basically the same diet he did as a young adult dog. Your dog could become obese and like humans this is a precursor to disease. This slowed or diseased metabolic rate, plus less exercise reduces caloric need as much as forty percent and at least by thirty percent. This in turn makes Fido's energy level decrease. An overweight dog has less energy just like an overweight human.

When you see these signs of aging in your dog, it most likely means you need to change the food he's eating. But many dog owners don't understand when their dog is overweight. Your obese dog is in more risk of bad health and it's like a yellow flashing light that's trying to alert you to this fact. Why would you not take notice and heed this warning? Numerous vets have found that pet owners tend to see their dog's weight as normal, though it isn't. Obese or not is a subjective opinion or they just see their dog as beautiful. They think that the weight is normal for their dog's size and view correct weight as too thin.

Besides knowing how much your dog weighs, knowing what body conditioning means is important. This is a better barometer of whether on not Fido needs to lose weight. It lets you know how your dog should look and feel to you. When your dog is at his ideal-weight you should be able to feel his ribs through his coat. They shouldn't stick out so that you can see their outline. When you look at your dog in sideways view, you should see a tuck in his abdomen.

You can find drawings online to help you understand what your dog's body conditioning is and how he should look when his weight is ideal, not too thin, or too heavy. He could also begin to lose weight as he ages because of a change in his metabolism, though that is more unusual. His metabolism is related to more than how his body processes his food. You'll want your vet to examine your dog concerning these health issues.

The Best Diet for Your Dog

There has been considerable debate as to the best food for dogs. People used to think that too much protein could cause kidney problems, but that has been proven wrong. Another point, commercial dog food manufacturers have improved their formulas over the years. The meat-based diets are better than in yesteryears. A meat-based diet according to some vets is the best if your dog is in normal health.

Here is the key to picking a good commercial dog food for a healthy dog.

Its protein content should be 30% or higher, fat at lest 15%, vitamin E and C should be the preservatives, and it should have some Omega fatty acids. Dogs can synthesize twelve alpha amino acids of the twenty-two that mammals need. They need to get the other ten in their diet and they are essential. They have short and basically simple gastrointestinal tracts and can't rely on microbe amino acid synthesis like herbivores, which have long gastrointestinal tracts and can produce amino acids via billions of microorganisms residing in their tracts.

They can use fats from plant and animal sources. Dogs can synthesize linoleic acid from lenolenic. Dogs use carbohydrates to fuel muscular and metabolic activities, though they can live well with fewer carbs and use more fat and protein. Good sources of protein for them are beef, chicken, fish, lamb, and meat by-products. Don't get upset by by-products. According to the Association of American Feed Control Officials the by-products don't contain hair, hide, hooves, or feathers. It refers to organ meats meaning liver, kidney, stomach, heart, blood, spleen—all of which dogs ate in the wild.

You should avoid feeding your dog commercial dog food that contains corn because it's hard to digest and causes lower nutrition and looser stools. Beef pulp has few nutrients and can make stools difficult for your dog to pass. Beware of preservatives as some are carcinogenic. Some companies don't like using vitamin C and E as preservatives because the shelf life isn't as long as with other preservatives and it costs more. Experts disagree as to what constitutes the best diet for your beloved canine friend. Some don't trust by-products and definitely want to avoid all meal in their dog's diet.

Even so, people who say that they need vegetables and fruits because they did eat a percentage of these in the wild agree they need meat. And it's best to avoid dog foods that just say meat and don't list any of the types of meat in the food. If you want the very best food for your dog and can afford it then what is called "real food" or "real food diets" could be the way to go. This food will normally be raw and is frozen or freeze dried. They are made to fulfill a canine's nutritional needs most of the time made from natural or organic ingredients. The best sources of dog food are natural food stores, veterinary offices, and some feed stores carry high quality food.

Your Dog and Oral Health

The oral health of your dog is more important than you may know. About eight percent of dogs over three years old suffer from periodontal disease. Their gums and bones that support their teeth are deteriorating. This is serious business. But good dental health can afford your dog two to five more years of life. This disease can cause other very serious diseases. This is because the bacteria from this oral disease can get into your pet's blood stream, when that happens it can cause infection or damage to your dog's kidneys, liver, heart or lungs.

Many dog owners don't inspect their dog's mouth, teeth and gums. Then when they take them to the vet for another reason they find out that their pet has loose teeth, sore and infected gums and rotting tooth sockets. That's when the owner may reply that they noticed that their pet has bad breath. The bad condition of the animal's mouth and gums creates toxins. Bad breath is a sign of these oral health problems.

The moisture and warmth of your dog's mouth along with nutrients make a great breeding ground for the bacteria. The bacteria starts out as normal and natural, but after plaque is present the bacteria grows at an alarming rate and it's out of control and has become dangerous to your pet's health. That's because the normal microbial flora is out of balance and pathogenic organisms have the chance to proliferate.

What are some of the diseases that can afflict your pet's mouth? First, there is periodontitis, which is the term for the overall diseased condition of your dog's mouth. It affects the gum, bone and delicate tissue. Gingivitis is an inflammation of the gums. Pyorrhea is an inflammation of the gums and tooth sockets. It can cause the teeth to loosen and pus to form. There can also be a decalcification of the tooth enamel called caries. It cause cavities, but this condition is rare for dogs.

Plaque can cause caries and calculi buildup and periodontal disease. Plaque is caused by material adhering to the enamel of teeth. The makeup of plaque is bacteria, salivary polymers, particles of epithelial cells and white blood cells. Tartar or calculus is deposits of calcium carbonate, and calcium phosphate that combines with food on the surface of the teeth.

One suggestion for keeping your dog's mouth healthy is feeding him with a well-balanced meat based diet. That keeps the environment of the mouth healthy. Getting your dog to chew treats is another good habit that can assist in keeping the mouth structures healthy. This will exercise his teeth as he chews a hard rubber, nylon or compressed rawhide chew. Brushing your dog's teeth every day helps, but less brushing doesn't. You must brush them enough to keep clinically healthy gingival maintained.

Evidence shows that soft diets promote periodontal disease. Harder foods that require more chewing helps prevent the disease. To help maintain your pet's oral health use these suggestions and ask your vet what else will help.

Your Dog and Toxic Foods

As with oral health diseases that create toxins that are harmful to your dog—so also there are foods that are directly toxic to him. Chocolate is one of the foods that are toxic to your pet. Large amounts of chocolate cause's coma and death. A smaller amount causes diarrhea and other gastrointestinal problems. How poisonous it is to your pet depends on how much your dog weighs the type of chocolate and the amount eaten. Chocolates that contain more theobromine are more toxic to him. Semisweet and bakers chocolate contain this compound. Dogs like chocolate a lot, but don't let your pet eat this treat. It can adversely affect the heart and nervous system.

Another food that is toxic to your dog is onions and avoid feeding him baby food because some contain onions. The disulfides sulfides can harm red blood cells. This causes anemia. Garlic causes the same problem. It doesn't matter if they're cooked; powdered or fresh they are bad for your dog. Mushrooms can cause shock and death. All are bad for him but some are more poisonous than others. The ones that grow in your backyard can hurt him and you should pull them up and throw them away.

Nutmeg can be hallucinogenic in large enough quantities. It isn't good for your dog to go through the trash because moldy food contains toxins and can make him ill causing vomiting and diarrhea and can affect other organs. Macadamia nuts are bad for dogs because they cause gastrointestinal problems, lethargy, stiffness, vomiting, and muscle tremors. Citrus oil extracts can make him sick causing vomiting.

Also, don't give him raw potatoes and the ones that have the green spots are worse. Nor should you give him rhubarb or tomato leaves or tomato stems. They contain oxalates that can harm the nervous, digestive, and urinary systems. All of these foods are poisonous to your beloved pet. So avoid feeding them to him or leaving where he may get them and eat them. There are foods that aren't toxic that are bad for your animal.

You should avoid feeding him cat food or leaving cat food where he can get to it because it's usually too high in proteins and fats for his digestive system to handle. Though not as likely that he would be attracted to them, coffee and tea are harmful to him in a fashion like chocolate. Fat trimmings and other fats can cause pancreatitis. Hops cause elevated temperature, faster heart rate, and death. Why is unknown. It isn't likely he'll ingest hops, but avoid the chance for him to ingest it.

Some adult dogs may not have enough enzyme lactase to handle dairy products. This causes diarrhea. You can get lactose-free milk products made for pets. Persimmons can cause enteritis and obstruction in his intestines and peach pits cause obstructions in the digestive tract. Raw eggs stop him from absorbing biotin because of an enzyme called avidin. This causes skin and coat problems.

Your Dog--Arthritis and Diet

Arthritis affects one in five dogs over the age of seven. And seven is the median age for when a dog is becoming an older dog. Of course, abnormal weight puts more pressure on your dog's joints. This causes more pain and swelling. In this case it's good to reduce the fat in your dog's diet. If your dog has arthritis he shouldn't eat foods with preservatives, wheat, soy, corn or food colorings. Most commercial dog foods have several grains in them and they increase inflammation, which irritates arthritis.

You can also give your dog a glucosamine and chondroitin table. It will help lubricate his cartilage. The normal dosage is a 500 mg tablet per ten pounds of body weight one time daily. MSM is an organic sulphur that studies have shown relieves arthritic pain, slows joint deterioration, and reduces inflammation. It hasn't any negative side effects. Since dogs don't usually get enough Omega 3's in their diets, give your dog a supplement like fish oil tablets to get these fatty acids. It helps reduce swelling in joints.

There are some recommended commercial brands to help relieve arthritis in dogs. Hill's (Rx/d) and Purina (JM Joint Mobility) are formulas made for this purpose. The most important joint supplements have been added to the dog food. If you decide to give your dog supplements instead, then go for the weight control formula because that will help his joints too.

These are some signs indicating that your dog is developing arthritis.

- Doesn't want to play, walk, run, climb stairs
- Doesn't want to be petted or touched
- Falling behind when you walk him
- Has a hard time getting up from a prone position
- Limps

Twenty-five to thirty percent of dogs develop joint disease. That is why it's so important to take notice of any of the signs that could indicate that your dog is beginning to suffer from any inflammatory illness. Joint disease is more likely in larger dogs and some forms are congenital in pure breed pets. If you see any warning signs take your dog to the vet and work out a health regimen for him.

These are the types of arthritis that plague dogs.

- Osteoarthritis
- Degenerative Joint Disease
- Hip Dysplasia
- Elbow Dysplasia

- Knee (stifle joint)
- Osteochrondrosis
- Hypertrophic Arthritis
- Shoulder Degeneration
- Wrist Arthritis
- Kneecap Dislocation

The choice to help your dog get relief from arthritis or to prevent it from developing is yours. As you can see there are several ways to keep your dogs joints healthy that you can utilize. Really it depends on how much time you have whether or not you would make your dog's food yourself, give him supplements, or feed him commercial dog food made to help treat arthritis. And definitely your vet's opinion on your dog's diet is a consideration. Many vets do recommend supplements and arthritis food formulas for treatment of arthritis in dogs.

Geriatric Dogs and Preventative Measures

Weight can be factored into the defining of the age at which Fluffy is geriatric. If Fluffy is under twenty pounds and her age is between nine and thirteen years old, she's geriatric, if she weighs between twenty-one to fifty pounds she's geriatric at nine to eleven years, and she's geriatric at seven to ten years if she weighs between fifty-one to ninety pounds. If Fluffy is a giant breed of dog, she's geriatric at six to nine years old and is over ninety pounds.

Two general preventative measures you can take to care of Fluffy when she is geriatric includes detecting diseases in their early stages and considering her risk factors like the characteristics of her breed, her environment, her diet, genetics, and amount of exercise. Her risk factors can influence her health by making her more susceptible to certain ailments. The last few decades has seen an increased lifespan for pets because veterinary science has made great strides. Here's what her vet can do to keep Fluffy healthy.

He can give her a full medical exam and make a complete medical history, do a complete blood count, biochemical profile, urinalysis, fecal exam, and heart worm test and give vaccinations. The common illnesses and disorders Fluffy may develop are obesity or weight loss, specific/special diet requirements, dental disease, arthritis, cancer, skin tumors, urinary problems, metabolism disease, prostrate disease in males (not neutered), endocrine disorders, cardiac disease, cognitive dysfunction, and behavioral problems. At home you can help Fluffy by brushing her teeth, grooming, feeding proper diet, controlling her weight, exercise her, and give her meds and let the vet know of any problems.

Geriatric Dogs and Heat Stroke

Another problem that geriatric dogs (along with puppies and overweight dogs) are more prone is heat stress. Pugs and Bulldogs are most likely to have heat stress issues because their noses are short and they already have trouble breathing and with panting. Also, dogs that have respiratory and heart disease may be more prone to heat stress.

Heat stress prevention measures are common sense and they are to never leave your dog in a hot car or any other hot closed place. If you have a kennel it should be well ventilated during summer heat. Always put Rover in a shady area outside during the summertime. In the summer season, don't exercise Rover too much. Always have fresh water for Rover when it's hot outside.

If Rover does get heat stroke, treat him and then take him to his vet because his vet should treat him for heat cramps and exhaustion. You need to treat him first because he could die or have brain damage occur if his body heat isn't quickly reduced. If his body heat reaches 106 degrees Fahrenheit he can sustain nerve damage within a few minutes. Do these things to cool him down.

• Slowly put in a container of cold water or spray him with a hose
• Put ice packs on his head and neck

- Put him in the shade if you are out in the woods and cool off his inner thighs and inside ear flaps using cold water

Old Dog Encephalitis

You may be wondering what is old dog encephalitis? This is a disease resulting from Fluffy having had distemper years ago. This is a persistent effect of brain inflammation from the distemper. Fluffy recovered from the distemper, but somehow she has a recurrence of the brain inflammation when she is old. These legions are equivalent to those that continue on to become a chronic neurological distemper as a part of the original distemper. What is distemper?

Canine distemper is akin to measles in humans. The distemper virus is enclosed with a fatty envelope, which is easy to upset in the surroundings or habitat. The virus must stay whole to infect Fluffy. She is less likely to get it from the virus being in her habitat. It would have to be very new to her environment. If it's in her environment over thirty minutes it isn't fresh enough to harm her. It also has to involve bodily secretions from an infected animal. So these secretions have to be left in her environment from another animal or she has to come in contact with an infected animal. If you make a habit of cleaning and disinfecting Fluffy's bedding and her sleeping area, this will kill any distemper virus infecting the environment. This virus is like any other, if frozen and placed in the dark it can live for years.

Usually the infection comes from an infected dog coughing or respiratory secretions. The virus is present in most other body fluids, even urine. It comes in through the nose or mouth and starts multiplying.

Then Fluffy's immune system surrounds the virus with macrophage cells. They are supposed to form a barrier because the virus is locked into the macrophage cell and the enzymes will kill the virus. But with the distemper virus this defense process is preempted as the virus uses the macrophage as a ride through Fluffy's body. The virus heads for her lymph nodes and makes it within twenty-four hours. It takes about six days for the virus to trek to her stomach, small intestine, spleen, and liver. At this point she has a fever.

A vital point in the development of the infection is reached in about eight or nine days. Fluffy's immune system has been constructing a defense against the virus during the duration of these days. Whether the virus or Fluffy's immune system wins round two is pivoting on the strength and swiftness of her immune system's attack. If her immune system starts to turn the tide then it'll clear the virus out by the end of day fourteen and Fluffy won't have any systems by then. If her immune system response is feeble, the virus will reach her epithelial cells, which lines the outside skin and the inner cavities. Epithelial cells also line the brain chambers and these will get infected too; they are delicate cells.

The spreading of the virus makes Fluffy sick, though if her immune system keeps mounting its attack the virus will decline. This actuality is responsible for ample diverseness in symptoms; while Fluffy may get many symptoms, Rover may only get a few of them. After Fluffy's immune system has cleansed most of her internal organs of the virus, the most sinister aspect of the virus may now take its toll; it may hang out in her skin and nervous system for a very long time. This actuality can cause calluses on her skin, but the more horrific aspect is it may cause seizures ages after you thought she was totally well from distemper.

In countries where dogs receive vaccinations there's less occurrence of distemper. If the mother has been vaccinated the puppies are better off and they get some immunity from the colostrums in her milk. They need their own vaccinations by age sixteen weeks. Tests for distemper can't be solidly verified because while a positive means Fluffy has the virus, ironically a negative test isn't definitive confirmation that she doesn't have it. The three types of tests for the distemper virus are the distemper antibody levels, cerebrospinal fluid antibody levels, distemper inclusion bodies.

Fluffy' immune system is her best defense against distemper. There really isn't a treatment for distemper. Some things can be done as adjunct

therapy like giving fluids to prevent dehydration if she has diarrhea. Your best strategy against old dog encephalitis is
prevention by vaccination and building up her immune system.

Prevention of Bloat

Bloat usually happens to middle aged and older dogs. Some estimates say that only cancer kills more dogs. It is seen more in deep-chested dogs like German Shepherds, Dobermans, and Great Danes. The medical name for bloat is Gastric Dilation-Volvulus. Rover could die before an hour has passed, if he has bloat. Get him to the vet quickly. If his vet doesn't have a twenty-four hour emergency line get the number to an emergency vet service and keep it where you can easily get it and call to say you're on your way with a dog that you think has bloat. It's advisable to keep a gas relief product handy to give Rover to relieve gas if you think he has bloat. The reason why is it could help save his life if he has bloat by adding extra time to drive him to the vet before the bloat is fatal.

Chapter Three: Making Your Dog Comfortable in Their Senior Years

Your Senior Dog's Behavior as It Gets Older

So Fluffy or King is getting up in years now and you're wondering what to do to make him more comfortable around the house and how to avoid or lessen different problems that come with an aging pet. Your aging pet is like an aging human being in that he or she has the right to set some of her own limits. In other words, your aging pet has been active and independent for years; though he needs extra care don't make an invalid out of him. Follow this rule as long as you can.

Fluffy or King has been a house dog for years or has sleep in at night. Now you're worried about incontinence. Still, it's best not to coax him to go outside and better to keep an eye on your pet to see when he's ready to go. That way King can avoid accidents and feel better about being in the house without being forced outside when he doesn't have to go and maybe his stiff bones make him want to wait a bit. He'll go to the door when he's ready. Understand that this means he's not senile enough yet to just do his business anywhere or hasn't lost bladder control yet.

You may have a situation where Fluffy nips at a toddler, say your grandchild that wakes her up suddenly. This is something that older dogs can't help and shouldn't be punished for it. The better solution is to keep toddlers and children away from older dogs. Give Fluffy a place to sleep that is secluded from the children. Keep in mind that Fluffy didn't behave like that when she was younger. Now her lungs aren't as efficient and her brain isn't receiving as much oxygen. This adversely affects memory and learning.

Her brain is undergoing changes just like human beings undergo brain changes as they age. Her brain is going through what in humans is called senile dementia. This is something that happens to dogs that are verging on sixteen years of age according to Professor Ben Hart of the University of California. He studied the aging process and concluded that in dogs it's very much like human aging. The reasons Fluffy may get angry when disturbed are that the messages aren't running along her nervous system to her brain as fast as they formerly did, and the blood vessels in her brain have lost elasticity.

King at sixteen years will become more disoriented, and bark for no reason. He may get stuck in corners, head for the wrong side of the door when wanting to go outside or just stare into space sometimes. These are problems that over seventy percent of dogs at that age have to cope with and having patience with his waning ability to handle himself in the house or outside in very important. When he first begins to age more he will probably follow you around more and be underfoot. Watch out for this so he doesn't trip you and he doesn't get hurt either. But with more age he will follow you less often and generally be less interactive.

You and your aging dog can still live together in the house and get along well. It's a matter of your ability to understand the changes he's going through and to adjust to them because he can't change what's happening to him.

Senior Dog Travel and Pet Sitters

When you plan a trip—that summer vacation or winter trek your senior dog will be more comfortable staying at home than in a boarding kennel or at the vet's in a cage. So if you must travel without your dear friend you'll need a dog sitter and one that can be trusted to treat your dog well. There are several questions to ask when hiring a pet sitter to ensure you get the best one for your dog.

One of the first questions to ask is whether or not the sitter is licensed and bonded. The pet sitter's insurance is similar to other insurance say the insurance a massage therapist needs when she runs her at home business. This insurance insures to pay if one of her client's has an accident while on her property. Pet sitter's insurance will pay for accidents that may happen to your pet or property, while you are away and the pet sitter is in your home. The next important question to ask is if the pet sitter is bonded. Good pet sitting businesses will be bonded. This insures that if the sitter steals some of your property while sitting your dog the stolen items will be paid for if the sitter is found guilty.

It's also a good measure to ask for local references that you can call and ask their opinion of the care the sitter gave their dog. It's also good to find out if your sitter will be signing a contract. What you want from the sitter can be spelled out in the contract. Another thing you'll want to do is to meet the sitter ahead of time. This way you can get to know the sitter a bit and see if you want her caring for your dog. It's also a chance to see if your dog and the sitter will get along well.

Many times when a pet owner reads that the pet sitter is licensed, bonded, and insured they think the sitter is licensed after taking a course in pet sitting. Though there isn't any professional licensing for pet sitters, she may have a regular business. Alternatively, many pet sitters take courses in first aid, dog training, and business courses that prepare them to be a better dog sitter. There are also private companies that offer pet sitting courses and your potential pet sitter may have taken such a course. But these are just helpful course for your pet sitter and legal requirements for running a pet sitting business.

When you go on that trip, following these measures beforehand to insure the comfort and safety of your dog and that your pet likes the sitter will be reassuring for you while you're away from him. Having someone take care of him that he likes will reduce his anxiety while you're away, whereas, leaving him at kennel or the vet's office, though he may be familiar with the people won't be like him staying in his own home where he feels the safest. Remember that senior dogs are more prone to anxiety attacks caused by separation from their owner and friend that they trust, than younger dogs.

More Advice to Help Your Older Dog Spend Their Silver Years in Comfort

If your senior dog has trouble with mobility caused by arthritis, hip displacement, loss of strength, then trim the hair around his paws that will aid in traction on slippery floors and install skid-free carpeting in spots where he lies down the most. Make sure it's always trimmed close. Also, you can put skid resistant socks on his paws. These measures will greatly aid your senior dog in getting up from a prone position and moving about the house.

Another option is to use the booties they issue people in hospitals and adapt them with Velcro in order to secure them tightly around your dog's legs. But be careful not to fit them tight enough to hurt your dog. Your dog isn't going to like having something cover his paws, so to get him used to the booties, try putting only one on at first. This will take some patience on your part because Fluffy may try to chew the bootie off or resist you in putting it on. Fluffy's bones are losing density if she is seven years old or older. Her bones will fracture more easily so these measures can help prevent those fractures. If one of her bones does get fractured it'll take longer to heal than when she was a young dog.

Fluffy's coat will thin with age and she may need a sweater. Also make sure her "bed" is in a warm spot in the house. Keeping her warm enough will relieve some of the pain and stiffness from inflammatory diseases. In the summer make sure she is cool enough, but not cold. If you remember seeing your grandmother suffer with swollen joints, then you have an idea of what your senior dog could be going through.

You may notice that Fluffy doesn't respond to your voice commands like she used to do. This could be a signal that she's losing her hearing. In this case you may need to use more hand signals to get her to understand what you want her to do and everyone in your house hold should start stomping when they are coming near her and she is sleeping. She'll be able to hear people approaching and won't be startled. That could save someone from being nipped. Also, she could become blind. If this happens, definitely don't rearrange the furniture and for rooms she normally goes in leave them open or she'll walk into them.

All of these measures may seem like a lot of trouble, but not more trouble than your canine friend is worth. Just as you've always cared for her health and happiness, you'll need to take special care in her twilight years. Memories of Fluffy when she was more active, playful and responsive to you are treasures you won't forget. Though her memory is waning she is still your beloved pet. When she can recognize you and other people she has loved she'll be delighted. When she can remember the house rules she'll feel better about herself. There'll be times though when she forgets the rules … have patience.

Setting Up Your House to Make Your Old Friend Comfortable

When your beloved pet gets older it needs a more comfortable living arrangement. The first thing you may notice is that his muzzle is graying. Your dog doesn't have as much energy as he used to and his bones are starting to creak. His teeth may have problems too unless he has had regular oral care. Larger breeds age faster than smaller breeds. There are large breeds that are old at five years. There are things you can do to help your senior dog live a happier life. But have your veterinarian examine your dog because the signs you're noticing may not be age related.

Now you can make your dog's living quarters easier for him to deal with. You can do things around the house like having fresh water available in different rooms so he doesn't have to walk as far and avoid having things he would want upstairs. You can avoid injury to your senior dog in the house by using rubber backed mats or rugs that will help keep him from sliding or falling on slick tile or waxed wooden floors. Placing cushy bedding in several areas of the house and especially downstairs, so he won't try to climb the stairs to your bedroom is a good idea. Climbing stairs for a senior dog can aggravate his arthritic condition and he may hurt himself in the attempt.

If your dog has always been allowed on the furniture like your bed or the couch then a set of pet ramps or doggie stairs will aid him in climbing onto your bed or couch. If he is having a hard time getting into your car folding or telescoping ramps are very useful and are sold in pet stores. You can reduce your large dog's neck and back with elevated feeders. This may be the best thing for him if he is arthritic. If he also has missing teeth or other oral problems then feeding him softer food and adding some water and mashing up his food can aid him in eating. It will also help his digestion.

For your senior dog with vision problems it's best not to rearrange furniture because he'll be able to cope better when he knows where the furniture is already. In this case, using baby gates to keep him from attempting to climb stairs is the best option. Your senior dog may have incontinence issues and if he doesn't have serious health related problems, then it's usually caused by an infection or age-related changes like hormone imbalance, loss of bladder muscle control, and weak bladder sphincter. If his problem can't be treated medically, then you'll need absorbent pads handy around the house. When you put them on your female they can be held in place with doggie bloomers and a male belly bands works well.

For older dogs with weak bladders a doggie door will help them not to mess up the house. This will make him feel better as he won't have to go in the floor and scolding your older dog for mistakes won't help improve the situation. All of these problems that you and your aging dog have to deal with are easily handled with a few sensible and kind precautions. So don't let it get you or your dog down for long. Your senior dog really needs your help and understanding. He's been a good friend for years…don't let him down when he needs you the most.

Adopting an Older Dog into a New Household

There are a myriad of reasons that older dogs are taken to shelters and it usually isn't for behavioral problems. Usually the dog is up for adoption for reasons that pertained to the owner not the older dog. Sometimes people get the idea that the dog is up for adoption because it's inferior in some way, but many pure bred dogs end up in shelters too. Here are some of the reasons that older dogs lose their homes.

Many times people buy a dog on an impulse or for some use like protection, if the dog's usefulness wears out or the owner just gets tried of caring for the animal, he may end up in a shelter. This is more problematic for older dogs because so many people want to adopt a younger dog, especially if they have children. A puppy has the knack of being cute and that is hard to ignore. Sometimes the dog's owner dies and leaves the dog companion behind and there isn't any family to take care of him or they don't want a dog. This situation is particularly traumatic for a senior dog.

It's harder for the senior dog to lose a home because he may not get another one. This can happen become the owner decides he doesn't have enough time anymore for his pet, the owners work schedule changes and he feels that interferes with taking care of his dog, such as walking him and is therefore afraid of accidents in the home, which are more likely with a senior dog. A new baby can be a reason for the senior dog to be ousted from his home. People are afraid that the senior dog will nip at the baby when it becomes a toddler and is not old enough to explain about not disturbing King while he's asleep. And King as a senior doesn't necessarily respond well to being suddenly awakened.

King's people may need to move and have to move where dogs are not allowed. So off King goes to the pound. Now he's feeling depressed and anxious for his owner to come back and get him, but that isn't going to happen. For a senior dog that may have health problems the stress of losing his home and felling abandoned can aggravate his ailments. The dog may be abandoned because the kids have gone away to college, he has allergies, or the new spouse doesn't like dogs. While you may wonder how someone could get rid of King for most of these reasons, it's a fact that it does happen and the parade of elderly dogs through shelters proves the sad tale.

If you would like to give an abandoned senior dog a new home consider these advantages of getting an older dog for a pet. Usually these dogs have been house trained, though while they are still upset they may not remember their training for a short period of time. But it will come back to them. They have already been socialized. They know how to get along with family members and in some cases cats too. They are companions ready to go walking and for car rides with you and will generally be good company, while not disturbing you when you are reading or watching TV. They've already learn not to chew your belongings and they know what no means.

An older dog who needs a home will already know how to behave in the house. You won't have to adapt the house for him like with a puppy, keeping things out of his way.

Chapter Four: A Few Things to Expect As Your Dog Ages

There are several diseases and ailments that your dog can have as she or he ages. Some of them are treatable, some of them you just make them as comfortable as possible until it runs its course. Like most diseases if caught early they can be treated and your dog will have a healthy, long happy life. That's why it is important to be diligent with your dog's veterinarian care such as their yearly checkup and as they age those checkups should include x-rays, urine screenings, blood work and anything the doctor orders in order to make sure your dog is in tip top shape for her age.

Here are just a few of the things to expect as your dog ages, they are ailments and diseases that are most common to elder dogs. Not all geriatric dogs will get one or the other of these ailments or diseases. Some people and their dogs are lucky and none of these things seem to ever bother their dog, however, you still need to be assiduous and bring your dog to the vet once a year even if you feel your dog is healthy there could be hidden signs to the disease or an ailment that you just don't notice.

Ailments and Diseases

Loss of hearing - your dog may experience the loss of his hearing as he ages. Dogs use many other senses to communicate with us besides their hearing. They know our patterns and continue to interact with us effortlessly so the first signs that your dog is losing its hearing would probably be he is walking into things or stumbling.

You can teach your dog hand signals, a sort of shorthand for sign language and they will respond well if you keep up the training and be consistent. One example is to use a flashlight to call your dog in from the yard at night; even during the day a dog would be able to see a flashlight.

Vision changes and eye problems - Nuclear sclerosis is common among aging dogs. It's cloudiness in their eyes and has little or no effect on the dog's vision. People sometimes mistake this for cataracts which do cause vision loss. An ophthalmic examination should be part of your dog's annual checkup. However if there are other problems with your dog's vision between checkups this could be a sign of some diseases and should be taken care of right away.

Canine Cognitive Dysfunction - CCD - More than half of the dogs over 10 years old will experience some form of canine cognitive dysfunction. This is characterized by behavioral problems ranging from confusion to changes in long-established behavioral patterns; one example is not making it outside to go to the bathroom. If you think you're dog might have CCD, talk to your veterinarian because there are new drugs to help some of the symptoms however it's important to rule out other causes first.

Canine dementia - As dogs age they become grayer, slow down and do a lot of the normal things that aging people do and sometimes that includes a form of Alzheimer's or dementia. This is characterized by aimless walking or pacing, a lapse in memory such as forgetting where to go to the bathroom or where they go to sleep at night. Some dogs even forget their name when they are called and might just sit and stare at you for a moment until they recognize their name again. A Canadian study shows that approximately 75% of geriatric canines experienced at least one symptom of senility by the age of seven.

Aggression - Some dogs as they age become more aggressive. In some cases aggression is a reflective action against pain. After having lost his vision or hearing your dog may snap or growl when he doesn't know where he is or bumps into things. The first thing to do is to find out what is bothering your dog, find the source of his pain. If you're dog's behavior suddenly changes take him or her for an exam at the veterinarian's office. If he is already on medication asked the vet if this could be the problem, such as behavioral side effects. If all else fails, and there is no pain found, you might have to consult with an animal behaviorists who specializes in dog aggression. They will be able to help you modify the dog's behavior to one of lesser aggression.

Loss of house training - some dogs lose their ability to go outside to eliminate waste when they get older. This could be a sign of a medical problem. Some such problems as they are holding it in for long periods of time are just too painful and they must go right away so they go in the house even though they know they need to go outside. You can help your vet with a diagnosis by writing down as much as possible about when the accidents occur and how often they occur and if there's a situation involved such as there is a child around or another dog present, when you had been gone for a long period of time or if it just happened. The vet will use this information in helping her diagnosis what is wrong with your aging pet.

Heart disease - such as congestive heart failure is much more common in elder dogs than in the younger dogs. Some dogs with heart disease will progress to heart failure while other dogs will never progress to heart failure and will stay at heart disease for the rest of their lives if treated properly. Doing something about heart disease is necessary in the prevention of heart failure. By supporting the heart and maintaining normal cardiovascular hemodynamic, there are medications that some doctors recommend, but they also have a variety of side effects.

One of the home remedies for heart disease is Omega-3 fatty fish acids which are basically fish oils. Other supplements to try and include co-enzyme Q-10, hawthorn, carnitine and taurine, and talk to your veterinarian about using these supplements, plus have your dog rechecked every three to six months.

Heartworm disease - This is a very treatable disease if caught early and prevention is the name of the game with heartworm disease. Even indoor dogs can benefit from preventative medicine. And heartworms don't discriminate against young and old dogs they can affect any dog at any time. Their eggs are transferred through mosquitoes and mosquitoes come inside as well as outside.

Kidney dysfunction - are also among the many ailments aging dogs face. Healthy kidneys keep in balance the body's chemical reactions, blood pressure, mineral levels, acid-base levels, and the elimination of waste products. Damage to the delicate and healthy tissue within the kidneys can eliminate them from contributing to maintaining homeostatic balance. There are a number of things that can cause kidney damage, such as bacterial infections, Lyme disease and common bladder pathogens. Fortunately a series of antibiotics taken over a period of several weeks will cure any infections but has the potential to damage the filtering system.

When it comes to kidney dysfunction be proactive, not reactive to it and ask for a urine test at every veterinarian visit for your dog to make sure you catch kidney disease before it causes irreparable damage. You can also be alert for frequent urination, increased drinking; dribbling of urine, even a trace of blood is a sign that your pet could have a kidney infection.

Periodontal disease - this is one of the most widespread diseases in dogs today. The tissue surrounding the dogs teeth, the gums and bones can become inflamed and infected. Having your dog checked biannually for tooth decay and gingivitis allows the vet to detect this condition much earlier and in turn and allows them to treat it more effectively.

Excess weight - excess weight on the geriatric dog can be extremely dangerous to the animal's health and well-being, just like humans. Their metabolism slow as the dog ages, they don't run around as much, they feel tired more often and would rather take naps than chase a ball. Just like humans, pets can suffer from *arthritis* or *joint problems.* Make sure they get enough exercise daily such as a walk or play time to help alleviate the extra weight put on their joints.

Exercise is important; however so it is diet. Don't drastically change your dog's diet without first consulting a veterinarian. You can slowly introduce a weight-loss food that will help your dog lose weight along with the exercise.

Synovial joints - the pain and stiffness most often associated with this joint disease - beginning of hip dysplasia and other joint diseases - is located in the synovial joints. Joints or articulations are physical structures uniting two or more bones. It is the articulation of the synovial joints that make it possible for us to bend our knees, move our fingers and our head and elbows; this is called the "true" joints. The progression of disease in these joints depends on whether the joints are freely moving or not.

Fibrous joints - there are three different types of fibrous joints and unlike the synovial joints are characteristic of having no joint capsule and little if any possible movement. The three characteristics are Sutures, Syndesmosis joints and Gomphoses joints. The most common joint disease found in dogs is *degenerative osteoarthritis* which is well represented by hip dysplasia. There are several other joint diseases including *Congenital* - which includes all birth defects of the joints; *Developmental* - occurring sometime after birth but before the bones mature; *Infectious inflammatory* - this type of joint disease is caused by an infectious blood-borne bacterial infection. *Neoplastlc* - although tumors of the joints are rare cancerous risks to the joints are possible. *Metabolic* - are the many genetic diseases of the joints. And finally, *Osteoarthrosis* - although they appear similar there are three different types of Osteoarthrosis, primary, secondary and the one that is most prevalent in older dogs is senescent arthrosis.

Idiopathic epilepsy - also called primary epilepsy, is a recognized symptom of epilepsy characterized by seizures over a long period of time for which there is no identifiable cause or cure. Many dogs with epilepsy or idiopathic epilepsy can live healthy happy lives in between the seizures. After seizure happens they become clingy to their main caregiver and have other changes in their behavior you might notice.

There are no tests for idiopathic epilepsy or other epilepsy however; there have been studies that show dogs with epilepsy have a higher level of a certain brain fluid when tested through the spinal fluid. During an idiopathic epileptic seizure, make your dog as comfortable as possible and allow the seizure to ride it out. It should only last a minute or two. You might have to clean your dog up a little because sometimes they lose control of their bodily functions.

Maximize the longevity of your dog

1. Take them for long walks, establish a routine exercise pattern with your dog such as two 10-minute walks each day, or even swimming which is great for arthritic dogs
2. Nutrition - be careful to feed the best quality senior dog food and be careful so they do not become obese. Some other herbal remedies for healthy living for your dog to ward off any possible diseases

3. Use antioxidants such as vitamin C, zinc, vitamin E, Omega-3 fatty acids and beta-carotene
4. There are some suggestions that hormonal agents such as DHEA and melatonin can have an affect on your dog's life spans

Old age in your dog is not a disease. When you're dog shows signs of illness it's not just old age creeping in it is a disease that can be treated if caught early enough. That's why it is so important to have your dog checked on a regular basis as they age so you can detect aging ailments and have them treated so your dog can lead a long, healthy life.

Chapter Five: Acupuncture, Acupressure, and Holistic Medicine for Geriatric Dogs

The majority of vets think that dogs live longer than they did previously. They say this is attributable to healthier diets, vaccinations whereby puppy diseases are eliminated, and improved health care. The caveat is because they are living longer they have time to develop geriatric illnesses. Acupuncture can treat many of these diseases. It is particularly suited for problems do to stress and chronic diseases. Many studies have proven that acupuncture works.

Acupuncture for Geriatric Dogs

Acupuncture has gained popularity as a treatment for dogs and particularly for geriatric canines. Though it is thought of as a newer alternative medicine in the west it has been practiced in the east for about 5000 years. A very early record of acupuncture treatments for an animal was in India and the patients were elephants. This was about 3000 years ago.

There are around 150,000 veterinarians trained as acupuncturist and about 700,000 assistants worldwide. The acupuncturist inserts extremely thin needles into specific parts of the body. Sometimes heat or a weak electrical current is also utilized in this healing art. Acupuncture causes the nerve endings to release more neuropeptides (endorphins) through stimulation. These endorphins are pain killers. It also releases natural hormones like cortisol, and neurotransmitters like serotonin. This treatment affects the central nervous system. It also boosts blood flow and lymph flow.

Make sure the canine acupuncturist is certified. Try to get a recommendation from your dog's vet. And only take your pet to one that has a good reputation. Take your pet for all of the recommended treatments. Try to keep your dog calm before the treatment. Be advised the illness may seem worse for two to three days afterwards.

Medically speaking, it can be used in three different ways. The first is as a primary treatment, the second is supportive therapy, and the third is a backup to a traditional therapy or treatment. The last idea is to use acupuncture when a traditional method needs help. It is particularly useful as an adjunct to medicine and surgery. It picks up the slack between the two. It is a complementary modality to other holistic approaches like massage, chiropractic adjustments, and homeopathic medicine.

Some of the diseases that are treated with acupuncture are gastrointestinal disorders, reproductive problems, respiratory illness, arthritis, allergies, obesity, and skin disorders. The effects of each treatment last for varying periods of time i.e.; from hours to days. The dog may show a good response to the treatment after only one session. Though it can take up to eight treatments to see improvement, but usually an effect is seen around the fourth treatment. The treatments can last up to thirty minutes, but sometimes they last only 10 to 30 seconds. How long it will take and how many treatments both depend on the disease and the dog.

Many times acupuncture works when anti-inflammatory medicine doesn't and it can be used effectively at times when surgery isn't recommended. There are certain situations in, which this therapy isn't recommended. For example, a very nervous dog can release enough adrenaline to stop the effect of acupuncture. Also, if a dog is being treated with certain medications, they can decrease the treatments benefit: three examples are corticosteroids, anticonvulsant drugs, and tranquillizers. Extreme caution should be used in the treatment of cancer with this method because if the wrong points are used the cancer can be stimulated to grow. These precautions are voiced by Allen Schoen, DVM. He is co-editor of "Complementary and Alternative Veterinary Medicine: Principles and Practice."

Other cautions can be raised: if the dog is pregnant and not prepared for labor, if a degenerative disease has progressed too far it can't be reversed by acupuncture, and some illnesses can only be treated by this method for relief of symptoms and as a supportive therapy. The American Veterinary Medical Association doesn't have a list of requirements at this time for vets interested in acupuncture therapy.

Acupressure for Geriatric Dogs

Acupressure is like acupuncture. But acupressure is a form of massage; it is like acupuncture minus the needles. When someone massages your dog with acupressure, they massage certain pressure points. According to both practices energy flow can be interrupted and that can cause organs to become weak. Thus, once the energy flow is working correctly, the illness will heal.

It is important to find a qualified practitioner. As the treatments continue, the practitioner will give your pet deeper massages. If he wants you to help at home, he will instruct you.

When your dog gets acupuncture treatments it helps him to give him acupressure treatment as a supportive measure at home. Sometimes dogs have a reaction to their pain meds and acupressure can help to relieve the pain of arthritis. If your dog has anxiety issues you can help him calm down with this method. You can also use it to increase his immune system's efficiency, to treat skin problems, and digestive ailments.

These are some of the benefits of acupressure massage: pain relief, lessens stress, helps immune system, can help detect illnesses earlier, boosts energy, improves blood flow to afflicted body parts, stop muscle spasms, and relieves stiffness. It can also make your dog's muscles, bones, and tendons stronger. Additionally, it causes natural cortisone to flow, which reduces swelling and inflammation.

Acupoint

Another type of treatment is acupoint therapy, started by Willy Penzel, which uses a therapy stick to press the pressure points, whereas acupuncture uses needles, and acupressure uses the vet's hands. There isn't enough evidence to concede that this method works as with the other meridian based modalities. Acupoint is mainly developing in Sweden.

Chiropractic Adjustments for Your Older Dog

The inventor of chiropractic for humans, Dr. Palmer, manipulated the spinal columns of horses too. But this treatment became unpopular around the 1930's. It has since been revived as a legitimate treatment for animals, including dogs. It was started again by Dr. Sharon Willoughby, vet and a chiropractor. She invented modalities of treatment that are appropriate and safe for animals. Since then, about forty years, animal chiropractic has utilized her work and techniques.

How does chiropractic work? The vertebrae of the spine are adjusted. That is, they are put back into their correct position. In other words, it treats musculo-skeletal difficulties. When one of them is out of alignment, it pushes against the muscle and many times pinches a nerve. Which diseases can be treated with chiropractic adjustments? These ailments include arthritis, muscle spasms, degenerative joint disease, intervertebral disc illness, and back pain. Many geriatric dogs can benefit from chiropractic treatments, but it is best to make sure that your dog is a good candidate for this modality. Sometimes the degeneration is too far along by the time an elderly dog is taken to a vet trained in chiropractic care.

Another way to explain chiropractic is to say that it corrects subluxations and that makes the nervous system work properly again. It actually is a remedy for the dysfunction, beyond treating only the symptom. When your dog's spine isn't in correct adjustment, blood circulation and nerve energy are impeded, which contributes to the development of various diseases. Energy and blood need to flow through the joints and organs. The pinched nerve is attached to an organ. All of this activity works in conjunction to promote health or to cause illness when this integrated system isn't working properly.

When these impediments are present some other types of deterioration happens including urinary incontinence, seizures, asthma, metabolic dysfunction, chronic vomiting, pain, problems with gait. Chiropractic treatments before your dog is older can help prevent the development of disease.

To be a member of the American Veterinary Chiropractic Association, the vet most have 150 hours of training.

Aquatic Therapy for Your Dog

Some animal hospitals now have aquatic therapy for your pet. It is a good therapy to use during the rehabilitation process. Since Fido is weightless in water this therapy can be started earlier than other therapies. Just as for humans, it is low impact exercise that is good therapy. It is a better therapy for obese patients and after operations of an orthopedic nature, and osteoarthritic dogs or ones with neurological conditions.

It is done with the use of an underwater treadmill or a swimming pool. The hydro-treadmill can be used earlier than other therapies. It is a safer therapy that helps Fido get his muscles back into shape and the warm water soothes his muscles. His range of motion is improved and his endurance is increased. Because he is exercising in water his joints aren't stressed as much by his weight. Thus, pain, inflammation, and tissue injury are lessened.

The underwater treadmills used are made for dogs and they are calibrated. Thus, resistance, speed and temperature are controlled to be suitable for a canine. The buoyancy is also controlled so that the individual dog is weightless. When the dog is weightless the bones and joints are decompressed.

So your pet can do more exercise, but feel less pain.

The belt of the treadmill moves in the water. Thus Fido can walk in his normal posture. The water level can be increased or decreased while he is walking. But more water equals more resistance. The speed can be adjusted so that he can start out walking, continue to running, and go to jogging. Hydrotherapy also gives your pet a psychological boost. When dogs are recumbent, not able to stand on their own weight without help it has a bad emotional effect on them. During hydrotherapy they can stand on their own and it makes them happier, which translates to recovering faster.

This is a very good way for older dogs to exercise. The resistance of the water and contact of the dog's paw on the treadmill promotes bone density. This is because it allows enough concussion, which is required to build bone density. It is good for conditioning in that it promotes cardiovascular health, develops muscles, it is relaxing, helps your dog attain peak performance, and it retrains his muscles.

Physiotherapy for Dogs

This has been used as a treatment for humans for quite some time, but it increasingly recognized as a treatment for pets. It is the use of physical techniques to treat injuries dysfunction of movement. Basically, getting their range of motion corrected to its original state or as close as possible. Your dog's vet should diagnose the problem first and recommend the therapy. You want the correct dysfunction recognized. Also, it is illegal for someone to treat your dog without his vet's knowledge and permission concerning the case. The law covering this is The Veterinary Surgeons Act of 1962.

Honey for Your Dog

According to some phytotherapist honey is good for dogs because it is good for the nervous system as a tonic, an excellent provider of energy, and it stimulates the heart. It is a predigested food because the bees have already digested it, which enables it to race directly into the blood stream. It also removes toxins and stops pathogenic bacteria from developing in the digestive system.

The honey that has healing properties is natural— unheated because heat kills about fifty percent of its effective properties. You can give it to Fido by putting it in his water. If he won't drink that, put it in a ball of food. Though this is about older dogs, note that it is given to puppies in milk.

Hippocrates actually used two honey based methods of treatment: water and honey and vinegar and honey. He treated many aliments with these solutions. There are also a lot of herbs to use to make tinctures with for various diseases. It is best to contact a trained phytotherapist that has experience in treating dogs. That way, your pet can get the right amount of the herb into his system—not to much, but enough. You should also inform your dog's vet of any herbal medications you are giving your dog. Some herbs could interfere with the absorption of a med or vice versa. Also, remember that herbs aren't totally harmless, if used improperly.

Your state may require him or her to be licensed as a vet before being able to legally give your pet treatment. Guidelines have been set by the American Veterinary Association for veterinary holistic medicine, acupuncture, chiropractic, and homeopathic medicine. You can find out from your state veterinary association, if a treatment you are considering is legal.

You may be interested in these Holistic Veterinary Associations.

American Veterinary Chiropractic Assoc.
www.animalchiropractic.org/

Academy of Veterinary Homeopathy
www.TheAVH.org

American Holistic Veterinary Medical Assoc.
www.ahvma.org

American Academy of Veterinary Acupuncture
www.aava.org

International Veterinary Acupuncture Society
www.ivas.org

Phytochemicals for Your Dog

Phytochemicals are found in many foods. There are in grains vegetables, and fruits. They are not nutrients. They do have some control over different processes of the body. Digitalis is one that doctors use to treat congestive heart failure and it is extracted from foxglove. Antioxidants are phytochemicals, but not all phytochemicals are antioxidants.

These are the phytochemical families: flavonoids, terpenes, plant sterols, indoles, polyphenols, phenolic acids, saponins, allyl sulfides, isoflavones, and isothiocyanates.

Alternative Therapy: Herbs for Geriatric Dogs

Many alternative therapies can help dogs live longer and healthier lives than modern, Western medicines. They can also treat specific diseases if you know the right combinations of the right herbs to distribute to the dog. Herbs are generally mild and can affect your dogs system simultaneously and act as a great, general body cleanser and body tonic. They are the ideal therapy for dogs whose physiology is not up to any form of severe stress, or for the animal that simply need to pick me up and they could be an additive for acupuncture or acupressure.

Many of these culinary herbs are gentle yet powerful tonics and provide high levels of antioxidants - substances which provide anti-aging properties. Some of these herbs include basil, oregano, turmeric, and thyme and any of the mints. And most herbs, in addition to the medicinal purposes, when sprinkled over the geriatric dog's food, will provide that extra little zest for their appetite when they may need it most.

These herbs have a whole menu of bioactive ingredients so any one plant might be helpful for preventing several specific diseases. One example is the dandelion root which acts as a diuretic and it acts as a tonic for the entire body but especially the urinary system and liver. Dandelion root is also known for its helpful properties against kidney and liver diseases.

Specifically for the heart is the hawthorn berry. This berry acts as a cardiotonic by enhancing the metabolism to include the heart muscles. These berries also help to strengthen the digestive system and the dog's appetite, as well as a great remedy for insomnia and nervousness. It's been said that "medicine is food and food is medicine" herbal medicines can be a valuable addition to an overall wellness plan especially for canine geriatric dogs.

These are a few examples of herbal remedies and nutrients used for treating dogs.

- Acidophilus, which is a form of good bacteria that keeps the stomach and intestines healthy, the good bacteria can be lessened by some medications, disease, and stress
- Alfalfa, which has phytoestrogens in it that help prevent cancer, osteoporosis, heart disease, and it helpful to the immune system
- Brewer's yeast: It helps to prevent shedding and aids in having a healthy coat and skin.
- L-Carnitine: an amino acid that is sometimes prescribed for dilated cardiomyopathy
- Chromium: It promotes better metabolism of fats, proteins, and carbohydrates.
- Kelp (Green algae): Has a cesium in it and it binds with carcinogens in the digestive tract and thus removes them. It also contains many minerals and trace minerals. Red algae: toxins and poisons from the intestine are absorbed by it, so they are excreted from the body. The chlorophyll content in blue-green algae is higher than any other plant, which is a purifier. They all have a large amount of digestible protein.
- Yucca: It is an ant-inflammatory and is also used for some digestive problems.
- Milk Thistle: used for cleaning the liver and it is prescribed for toxicity from pesticides, certain drugs, and poison mushrooms.
- Ginseng: Used for treatment of weight loss due to cancer, infections, nerve disorders, and

wounds. These are the side effects: edema, sleepiness, and muscle tension.

According to Michael DYM, D.V.M, in the 1960's many diseases in pets that vets see today were very rare back then. He says that over a forty year period this change has taken place. He attributes this horrid decline in the health of our pets to the lowered immunity of our pets. He states that their immune systems aren't what they use to be. He explains that these illnesses include "chronic skin/ear allergies, digestive upset, thyroid/adrenal/pancreatic disorders, seizures, gum/teeth problems, degenerative arthritis, kidney/liver failure, and cancer across all ages and breeds."

The list doesn't stop there because emotional and behavioral problems are also on the rise. He continues that it is analogous to the immune and behavioral illnesses that have increased in children. His explanation it that vaccines have been overused for pets, bad nutrition, and toxins. Plus, the usual treatments have only addressed the symptoms and not the actual causes of the ailments.

Thus, holistic vets consider and treat the immune system by boosting it so it becomes more efficient. They think of how to build a better defense system for your pet's body. Whereas, using antibiotics for example is an offensive treatment that fights an infection that has already invaded the body, but a holistic method would build a defensive fortress by improving your pet's immune system.

A main difference between holistic medicine and allopathic medicine is that the latter suppresses the symptoms for a quick relief, but the real problem isn't addressed so that itchy skin that was relieved by the allopathic method may go away, but the next stage could be diarrhea. Both symptoms in this scenario are related to the real underlying breakdown of the body. But the usual vet using the allopathic method may not see that the two problems are related and may only treat the symptom once again. This is the opinion of Dr. Jeffrey Levy, DVM.

According to Dr. Bernstein, DVM says that though allopathic medicine is a major cause of symptom suppression, using "herbs, acupuncture, and incorrect homeopathic remedies can also be suppressive." The idea is that all types of treatments have to be used correctly by someone skilled in their use.

Augmentation Therapy

It is also known as orthomolecular medicine uses large amounts of vitamins and minerals for preventing pathology, remedying nutritional deficiencies, and healing damaged tissue.

Homeopathy

The system of homeopathy used currently was started by Samuel Christian Hahnemann in the middle 1800's. He was a medical doctor. It revolves around the idea that "like cures like." For example, a diluted, small dose of a poison/toxin can cure, but a large amount, say that is swallowed by a dog can kill him.

Homeopathic doctors make their remedies from animal substances, drugs, plants, viruses, and minerals. They say that these treatments treat the real cause, not the symptoms.

Holistic Veterinary Medicine

Practitioners of holistic medicine use the least invasive philosophy to judge how to treat illness. This approach also thinks of the animal in his environment, considering every aspect thereof. They look into your pet's personal history and family history, his diet, any stress factors, and exercise. A holistic vet will try to stay away from the blood test and other technological methods. It incorporates all of these methods: botanical medicine, massive therapy, acupuncture, acupressure, chiropractic, homeopathy, nutraceuticals, and physical therapy. It also includes surgery and conventional medicine if necessary.

There are other terms for holistic veterinary medicine; they are complimentary veterinary medicine, integrated veterinary medicine and alternative. In the U.S. sixty percent of the schools for vets have some alternative veterinary medicine classes.

Physiotherapy for Your Dog

First, a veterinarian has to make a correct diagnosis before any physiotherapy can start. This is also binding by law that it is illegal without the consent of the vet treating your pet for anyone else to give any treatment of that particular case. This is according to The Veterinary Surgeons Act of 1962. (in England) After the vet has determined the extent of the injury and treated it, then the physiotherapy rehabilitates your dog.

Physiotherapy is well established in the treatment of humans after a car wreck for example and rehab is necessary. They also treat animals after surgery. Dogs are one of the main species of animals being treated with this therapy. These therapists treat musculo-skeletal injuries and ailments. It is becoming an important adjunct treatment for animals with injuries and dysfunctions in their ability to move. That is when their range of motion is limited by trauma. These are some of the problems animal have that are treated with physiotherapy: tendon injuries, back pain, joint and ligament injuries, wounds and lick granulomas, paresis and paralysis, osteoarthritis, hip and elbow dysphasia muscle imbalance, and atrophy.

There are several techniques that physiotherapists can use. Some of these techniques are: hydrotherapy, simulated laser, thermotherapy, ultrasound, acupressure, pulsed magnetic field, soft tissue and joint mobilization, neuromuscular stimulators, myofascial release, trigger point release, and certain specified exercises. The physiotherapist will decide which of the therapies your pet needs.

Some of the soft tissue problems addressed are: muscle strain, atrophy, and tightness. Treatment for the tendons and ligaments include tendons and ligaments that are ruptured and sacroiliac injury. In the orthopedic area they treat arthritic pain and decrease degeneration of joints. They also assist in healing wounds and fighting against bacteria.

The physiotherapist will endeavor to reduce pain, improve strength and flexibility, increase range of motion, and to stop another injury from occurring. Some types of pet insurance cover physiotherapy. The United States, Australia, and England are involved in further advancing animal physiotherapy. There is also an animal physiotherapy association in South Africa. You must be trained as a human physiotherapist before becoming one for animals.

Canine Bowen Technique

Another technique that is also used for dogs is the Canine Bowen Technique. It was first developed for people, but Sally and Ron Askew have developed a branch of it for canines. They are both students of the Bowen Technique she is also a member of the Pet-Dog Trainers Association of Europe. Sally also belongs to the Essential Oil Therapists for Animals guild.

It works through vibrations in the muscle. The therapist does certain moves causing the nerve ending to detect these vibrations. The nerve endings transmit all of this to the brain and the brain deciphers the information, which causes it to untangle any abnormalities. The therapist must be calm and caring. This persuades the dog to trust the therapist. The dog responds to the treatment while it is ongoing. Some of his responses are moving to another part of the room and then after lying there for a few minutes coming back to the therapist, nibbling, licking or just looking at parts of his body that the therapist finished treating. His coat may become dull and then be shiny at the end of the treatment. Also, his eyes may cloud and then clear up.

Training for Alternative Therapies Used to Treat Dogs

These schools located in the United States offer training in massage, physical therapy, and natural health treatments for animals: Southwest Institute of Healing Arts, Bancroft School of Massage Therapy, and the Center for Massage and Natural Health.

These are the days of enlightenment in animal health care. Many veterinarians are trained traditionally and in alternative therapies. There are more resources now than ever that can help you keep your dog in very good health and rehabilitate

Fido if necessary. This means that your older dog has a better chance to recover from illness or injury today that was possible in the past.

Chapter Six: Aids for Your Dog's Movement and Longevity

Many older dogs need help being mobile because of numerous different reasons such as arthritis in their knees and joints, perhaps a hip displacement or even an amputated leg. There are a number of harnesses and dog wheelchairs out there so that you can help your dog to walk and live a full, normal lifestyle as he or she did before.

It's not uncommon for elderly dogs or injured dogs or handicapped dogs to lose the use of their back or front legs. Nerve damage, DM (degenerative myeopathy), cancer, arthritis, accidents and other devastating diseases can all cause the loss of dogs back legs. Fortunately this does not mean the end of a dog's life. Dog carts and dog wheelchairs can offer for a new lease on life.

A Few Ideas to Help Your Best, Now Old Friend

Traction - trim the pads of your dogs feet as close as possible and keep them that way. This will give your dog more traction on slick floors. You may want to put down carpet squares where your dog normally lies so to be easier for him or her to get up and down for naps.

Another helpful idea for traction for your beloved aging dog is booties that help them with traction in all weather especially in the snow and on hardwood floors. These booties are machine washable and reusable and most dogs don't mind wearing them once they get used to them.

If you can't afford a dog wheelchair or a dog carts here are a couple of ideas that you can use that are a little easier on the budget.

- If your dog is having a hard time going down the steps with her front legs, place an old T-shirt on her front legs and then hold the back of the T-shirt while she walks down the steps, pulling up and back so as there is not that much pressure on her legs as she descends the steps.
- Unzip the vinyl brief case all the way around and then lay your dog on top of it and then use the handles to help walk the dog around just like the expensive dog harnesses you see in catalogs and on the Internet. If you believe the zipper is bothering your dog cut the zipper out of the briefcase and it works just as good.
- Use a canvass log carrier and lay your dog inside that as you would with a vinyl briefcase and then use the two handles to help your dog walk, this also works just as good as the high price harnesses or slings.
- Swimming is always a helpful idea for dogs with arthritis even a small galvanized 4 foot deep pool can have your dog swimming and helping her arthritic legs and joints for exercise purposes without hurting your budget.

Pain Medications and Treatments

With dogs living longer and longer, there ailments are growing and many have lived in pain for longer periods of time. But the advancement in pain medication has proven to be very helpful to many geriatric dogs. These new medications help dogs live a more comfortable, longer life than ever before. Medication along with treatments such as water therapy and acupressure or acupuncture can give an arthritic dog a new lease on life. These medications are also valuable for pets that have terminal illnesses that may last many years.

Slings and Harnesses

A sling harness is one in which a soft material is placed on the belly of the dog and then comes up around each side and it usually has handles to which you can help hold up the dog as you both walk. This gives the animal more of a feeling of independence. They make the straps long so that it won't hurt your back when you are walking your dog. It's almost like a carrying case for your dog.

There are harnesses and supports slings which fit around the back end of your dog and offer support to a dog that is not totally disabled but needs help walking. The handles offer the support while she does the walking. A sling is usually just small strips of leash that go around your dogs legs and up to the back and are securely held with a clip like those found on the dog's collar or a round ring, however a harness uses larger pieces of sturdy material and holds more of the dog and this is probably more comfortable for the dog but not all dogs like this.

It's a trial and error when it comes to the sling or the harness. You might have to try both before your dog is comfortable with one or the other. And you will have to get used to walking around with your dog, holding the harness or the sling at a higher level than you regularly reach. This is to help support the dogs back legs.

There are also harnesses and slings specially made for those animals that have had an amputated appendage. These are custom made to fit your dogs that are now physically challenged yet still wants to run about and play with the other dogs. The specially made harnesses and slings are designed so that the pet owner does not injure themselves while walking with a handicapped dog because it is very easy to become off-balance when the dog becomes off-balance therefore both of you could come tumbling to the ground.

Dog Wheelchairs and Carts

There will come a time when the sling or a harness just won't work and that is when you will need a wheelchair for your dog. Most dogs, after a day or so, really enjoying the rejuvenated speed they experience in the wheelchairs that they have been missing.

Dog wheelchairs are different than people wheelchairs. Most dog wheelchairs are for their hind legs and they use their front legs to propel themselves forward. Dogs can still do all the same things they love before they were put in a wheelchair or cart such as fetch, go hunting with their owners, swim and go for long walks. They get used to the wheels in the back pretty quickly and find that they can go a little faster than their friends.

Many older dogs that were not injured use a support sling cart to get around and most will enjoy it after a couple of days. Because if they have trouble with their back legs or their back they will find that this will ease the pain and they can run as fast as they want without adding pressure to where it hurts them.

The support sling dog carts and wheelchairs are assembled from links of sturdy aluminum tubing and connected with locknut bolts. A soft, gender specific, harness or saddle sling is worn by the animal and click securely to the frame of the wheelchair or cart.

The dog wears a comfortable harness that connects to the front of the wheelchair or cart. You place the harness on the dog before putting it into the cart. There are additional belly straps for additional support that are recommended to help support their mid-back or abdominal muscles. This is especially good for long dogs, dogs with mid-upper back injuries and older dogs.

Front support extensions are available for the wheelchairs and carts for dogs with a weak front leg issues such as dogs who have had strokes or those with arthritis in all legs. It's called the Quad training wheels. They are placed on the back of the dog wheelchair to give the dog extra support when running around.

If you don't get your dog a wheelchair through a veterinarian or supply store in your area, there are several places on the Internet you can purchase them from. There are about 10 different measurements you need to take on your dog so that they can send you the proper fitting wheelchair or cart specifically for your dog.

There are many reasons why a dog may need a wheelchair or cart. Some of these reasons are degenerative myelopathy (DM), disc disease, hip dysplasia, ruptured discs, spinal cord injuries, fractured backs, cervical disc disease, nerve degenerative, neuropathy, ACL, wobblers, tumors, cancer and chronic leg weakness among several other things that could be wrong with dogs legs and joints requiring them to use a wheelchair or cart to get around.

Chapter Seven: When it is Time to Say Goodbye

Dealing With the Loss of Your Dog

Eventually you will have to make a decision and stop the suffering of your beautiful, beloved pet because no one needs to live in pain. And that is one of the hardest decisions you will ever have to make, unless somehow your beloved dies in her sleep, you will have to decide when to put your dog down.

People will say they put their dog to "sleep" instead of saying they had to have their dog euthanized. It makes them feel better to say they put them to "sleep" because this terminology is part of the denial of what you are really doing and it is so difficult and it brings up all sorts of questions such as "Did I do the right thing?" "Was it time?" "Did I wait too long? Or make the decision to quickly?" "Did my pet suffer?" Some of these questions can be answered by your veterinarian. Or you can express these questions to a grief counselor or a pet loss support group.

Euthanasia

The more you know about euthanasia the better you will feel about your decision to use euthanasia as a kind way to help your dog end his or her suffering. Many people have stated that it is the kindest thing they've ever done for their pet. You can take your time in most cases and your vet will tell you how to make your terminally ill pets as comfortable as possible while you weigh your options. And never hesitate to ask the veterinarian what he or she would do if it were their dog. They might opt for the medication route versus euthanasia.

Tune in to your pet even if your pet is in a coma or is on continual medication; know that you will be anxious and upset and that your pet will be the same because they often reflect our emotions. Most people say that they waited too long, or they did it too early, and the fact is when it comes to death, unless it comes naturally there is no right time. Learn all you can about euthanasia and what to expect. Ask the veterinarian what her procedures are and to explain what will be happening to your dearly loved dog. It usually starts out with the veterinarian giving your dog a calming tranquilizer and once that takes effect, she will administer a lethal dose of anesthetic, something such as Phenobarbital. Your pet will then fall into a deep sleep and within about a minute their heart will stop beating, and they lose all the breath in their lungs, something like a sigh and it's over.

Cremation versus Burial

Since your pet is part of your family and your longtime companion, it is only natural that you want the best for him or her in death as you did in life. Many people are opting for cremation so they can have the ashes with them either at their home or to be scattered about the property so the animal is finally free. There are beautiful urns that represent every breed of dog and some of the most popular urns are ones that hold a photo of your beautiful pet. There are also tiny urns that you can carry with you so that a part of your pet is always with you.

Cremations run anywhere from approximately $100 and $120 to $300 depending on the size of the animal. And the urns cost in the range of $25-$100 for the average urn, however the custom-built urns, such as the ones in the shape of your pet, have no ceiling price.

Pet burial is a hard thing to do for someone who loved their pets so dearly. For "pet people" some of them have a hard time distinguishing flesh from fur because this has been their constant companion and confidant for years and years and now it's time to say goodbye it's been one of the toughest times of this person's life. And they need to be treated with respect and dignity. And that's what many pet cemeteries give them.

Many pet cemeteries offer burial services along with a memorial service at reasonable prices which means you can come and visit your pet whenever you like to put flowers and little trinkets at the gravesite. A burial is for people who like to have some where to go to visit their best friend instead of seeing them in ashes.

Grief and Grief Support

Guilt is a universal feeling when dealing with the loss of your long time companion. People such as friends and family don't understand that you've been the primary caregiver for this "family member" and taking care of its every need just like a child. And now you are responsible for the ultimate decision, to put it out of its misery and send it on to the heavens. And that adds a whole other layer of grief and guilt. We don't "put down" our friends or family members but we are forced to do this for our very best friend. It's heartbreaking.

Data has shown that many more people than one might think are devastated by the loss of their pet then the loss of a close friend or relative because the pet is with them 24/7, never leaving their side, never giving them any grief over anything. They are with you for such a long time that they are not just animals; they become part of your family.

When you have to deal with someone who has lost a pet, a sense of normalcy and sensitivity is of the utmost importance. Please don't say "it was only a dog" or "you can always get another dog" because people have lost their best friend don't want to hear that. When you've spent every day of your life with this companion, they cannot easily be replaced. You must be patient with your friend because it could take months even years to fully get over the grief of losing one's best friend and companion. Especially if that companion died of old age which means they were with them for a very, very long time. They may become withdrawn and not want to go out as much but allow them their grieving period, however long that may be.

If you have lost your pet, one idea would be to join a pet loss grief support group. Check with your veterinarian to see if there is one located in your town or city. A loss grief support group for pet owners will help you share your stories and give you a place to be heard and help you with the grieving process with others in your situation or who have recently gone through the same pain. Because unless someone has gone through what you're going through they don't understand.

Well-meaning, but often misdirected friends and family say things like "you can always get another dog." And they don't understand that you can't replace a loved one that easily and this often makes you wonder if it's right to grieve for your lost pet. And the answer is yes there are grieving periods and a grieving process that everyone should go through including those who have lost a beloved dog. After sharing so many life experiences with this friend, how can you not grieve for its loss?

When you've been with an animal for a long period of time and then that animal dies, it triggers a grief reaction just as it would anyone who grieves for anyone or anything, it is no different. Grief is grief and you must feel it in order to get over it. When you go to an animal grief support group there will be no one telling you "look, it was just a dog." Because they have all gone through the same thing you are going through at one time or another and they are there to help you.

Grief is a very individual process and can extend for many years. What helps in these animal grief support groups is having someone listen and not try to fix the problem immediately. Be patient if you're feeling the grief and pain for your beloved dog. You will get through it but it will take time.

Ideas to Help You through Your Grief

- Saying goodbye - take time for this, let the dog know how much she or he meant to you in your own way. If you're a writer or poet, use your talents as an outlet for your grief and anger for what is happening. Try saying goodbye while the dog is still alive. If you have to euthanize the dog, asked the vet as many questions as you have that's what they're there for and don't think any of them are silly.
- You have just lost one of the closest relationships you have ever had, let yourself grieve and don't be embarrassed by intense feelings.
- If you're not a writer or poet take a pottery class or some kind of creative

class where you can release your pent-up energy in a creative nonviolent way.

- Talk about your feelings this is where an animal grief support group would come in handy because they know what you are going through and they won't try to fix things by saying get another dog. There are also pet loss counselors or therapists that can help you if you're still grieving and don't feel that the support group is helping you.

- Hold a memorial service and it may just be yourself who attends but at least it puts some closure to the idea of your pet being gone. And if you're able to bury your dog in the backyard it's a great place to visit your beloved whatever you think of them. Or you can choose a pet cemetery where you can go and visit them as well. But a memorial service puts a closing on the situation and helps you with your grieving process just like with humans.

- Hold the party for your close friends who have dogs as a sort of celebration for your beloved dog. Obtain a wish list from the local animal shelter and have each person attending the party bring something from the wish list and then donate everything to the animal shelter in the name of your pet.

- Give the gift in the memory of your beloved dog. A gift to the local Humane

Society or pet rescue center this will also help you to grieve because you are doing something in the name of your beloved dog.

- Plant a tree in your yard for the memory of your beloved pet if you had them cremated or buried in the pet cemetery so the tree will always remind you of their love.

One must come face-to-face with the grief before they are ready to deal with it. Then they are able to talk about it and eventually they will be okay remembering the good times which are always the hardest part.

Greif Counselor or Therapist to Help You Through This Trying Time

If you decide to go to a therapist or a grief counselor, first make sure you're comfortable with them because not all grief counselors or therapists are the same and believe in the same treatment regimen. It's important for the grief counselor to provide you with support but they should also educate you about the grieving process telling you that the shock and numbness, yearning, searching and disorientation are all necessary and appropriate responses to the loss of your beloved pet and the grieving process. This can also lead to a reorganization which will lead you to a "normal life" without the pressures of a pet. For as long as you want to feel like you don't want to care for another pet. (See when to get a new pet). Of course the memories will never go away and there will always be some level of sadness, however, you do not want it to consume your life and that is where the grief counselor or therapist comes in. And the pain does go away but it takes time and only you are the one who can determine how long that time will be.

Pet Grief and Your Children

Grieving over a family member or close friend is no more important than grieving over a beloved pet when it comes to your child because to a child the pet is part of the family. However society doesn't always acknowledge the grieving of children when it comes to pets, they seem to brush it under the rug and think they will forget about it. But the bereaved child can have a whole host of things go wrong in their lives because someone ignored their grief. Things such as depression, anxiety, social withdrawal, underachievement at school and behavioral disturbances are all signs that they have not process their grief when a family pet has passed away.

Children and adults process grief differently, for example one study showed that children still had major depressive episodes up to one year after the passing of a pet. Without the proper help with grieving, children will develop complicated grief symptoms.

Some research has concluded that there are gender specific variations on grief when it comes to pets with young girls having more intense grief then young boys. Furthermore, the grief from a pet dying can bring up unresolved grief issues from a family member or close friend who has died if that child has experienced death before the pet has died. Sometimes children will feel more guilt because they feel greater grief when their beloved pet dies then they did when a relative had died. And this greater grief only adds to their guilt and makes it more difficult to grieve and so sometimes they act out or they become antisocial like not wanting to go to school because they missed their beloved pets so much, or they are so depressed over the situation that they just do not want to do anything.

Grief counseling for children is the best way to go when the family pet dies because children are complex and have years ahead of them that can be damaged through grief at an early age. They need someone who is trained in grief counseling to help them talk through what is bothering them and help them work out their feelings especially depression and anger which seem to go hand in hand after a beloved pet has passed away.

The Final Word about Grief

The death of a beloved pet can be a life-changing situation and the impact varies from person to person and across the wide continuum of responses. However these responses are similar to those experienced when someone loses a human companion and should be felt to their fullest. It is important to surround yourself with an environment that is supportive and understanding, such as the support group for grieving pet owners. Or to seek counseling to help with adaptive coping mechanisms if you feel you cannot deal with just a support group.

Try not to be apologetic for your grief to friends and family because you must feel what you are feeling, and that is grief, in order to honor the memory of your dearly departed companion. Whether they will understand or they won't is not your concern. Your concern is to be good to yourself, take care of yourself, and do what you can do to get through the grief process because it is a process. Seek help if you need it, there is nothing wrong with getting help, and it always makes you feel better.

Remember, the definition of euthanasia means a painless death to end physical suffering in an animal friend. It truly is the last gift we can give them.

When to Get a New Dog

Wait until you feel normal again before entering into a new relationship with the new dog. And don't think for a moment that you're being disloyal to your beloved dog by opening your heart to another dog. No dog will ever replace the one that passed away. You're not replacing your beloved dog there will never be a replacement for the dog you lost. Treasure the memories of your old pet and when you're ready, open your heart to a new and different relationship with another good friend.

Resources for Grief

Visit http: //epets.ca/memorial/support/ for grief pet support groups through the Internet.

Or you can call 800-869-6898 which is the Delta Society, a nonprofit group devoted to the animal/human bonds. They will provide you with a useful resource catalog including videos and books on pet loss and state-by-state listings of local pet loss counselors or support groups.

Chapter Eight: Our Dogs

FiFi - My Childhood Friend – Gina Stewart

Over my lifetime my family has owned several dogs; however I never felt any of them were mine except for one, FiFi. My parents purchased FiFi when I was only six months old so we grew up together. A medium-sized, black Poodle, she was my best friend. The only one I trusted and who seem to love me unconditionally in a growing family of uncertainty.

We have countless pictures and home movies of me growing up with my best friend and then adding my two sisters who never really cared much for FiFi. And that was always okay with me because it was two against two, well one human and one dog against two snotty little girls who would throw snowballs at my best friend when I wasn't looking. And then along came the Boxers. Mom started raising Boxers when I was about five years old and even though the puppies were cute and cuddly, I remain loyal to FiFi. My sisters each got a cat that year.

FiFi and I did everything together in our small town. When I rode my bike, she'd run along with me, when we play cowboys and Indians with the neighbor kids, she'd always play my horse albeit a tiny one. We'd hunt for fossils and four leaf clovers together in the front yard and she would help me dig for buried treasure in the sandbox in the backyard. She was my Eskimo dog in the winter and the greatest swimmer in the summer. She loved playing in the pool with us and didn't mind getting wet unlike the Boxers who wanted nothing to do with the water.

FiFi slept with me every night and I told her all my secrets and dreams, she never told anyone and I appreciate that to this day. She was the bestest, best friend anyone could ever ask for. Even if I didn't know what she was saying half the time, I didn't care. We had a special bond that was unbreakable.

She could not go to my dance recitals, spelling bees and other such indoor activities. However my mother did bring her to the football games where I was a small cheerleader for the peewee football team. And it was great to see her there all the time. She seemed like my own cheering section.

FiFi was there through the divorce of my parents when I was only ten. And I was too busy with my crying to notice that she wasn't moving as gracefully as she used to be. The move from Dayton to St. Louis was difficult on all of us but FiFi never seem to complain, she was still there for me. When I didn't know a soul in the new city and school she was right there for me. I talked to her for hours and hours and she just sat there listening and never closing her eyes, knowing exactly what I was saying. The fact that she never closed her eyes told me she was listening to me and that was so special to me.

Our new yard was smaller and we never seem to find any four leaf clovers and there was no place to look for fossils, no sandbox either. I was done playing with the neighbor kids, I was too old for that but FiFi would never grow old she would always be the same age and that was the age of the summer I was seven. We just had the best time ever that summer. It wasn't one specific thing, it was just a great summer and she was so spry and young, she would always remain that age.

When I began to make friends she was still there when I came home, waiting to hear all about my day or my night. FiFi was there with every boyfriend and broken heart, and my first article in the school newspaper, we celebrated with extra dog treats that night. She slowed down a bit more but was still excited to see me, and she needed a little help getting up on my bed but I still thought she would live forever.

I just turned 15 when I started working for an animal hospital several miles from our home. I had wanted to become a veterinarian when I grew up because I loved all animals, especially dogs. What I wasn't prepared for was the sadness of being a veterinarian. Or rather the veterinarian's assistant which is what I started out as.

Of course I was only cleaning up the kennels at first. But then I moved on to assisting surgeries and giving vaccinations, testing for heart warms and other diseases that people don't realize until it's too late.

Assisting in the surgeries was my favorite part of working at the animal hospital. I never fainted, and surgeries never grossed me out. And I was proud to say I stood tall while vet students from the university were falling like flies. The assistance I gave in surgery was to hold my fingers over the tiny hearts of the dogs and cats while they were sleeping to make sure that they were still beating. I thought that was the most important job, to make sure their little hearts were beating and to alert the doctor if they ever stop.

I took FiFi to work with me on occasion so she could see the other animals and get her own vaccinations and a bath or two. After all, I was a champion at giving dogs and cats' baths although it wasn't easy.

I'd been wrapped in my own world, doing my own thing expecting FiFi to be there at that same age she always was in my mind. What I hadn't noticed was that she was no longer black, but a dull, grayish color, and her life existed of sleeping most of the day and she was no longer happy to see me when I came home from school or work.

I was not naïve. I knew what was going on, she was 16 years old, almost 17 and she was in pain. I took her to the animal hospital with me for a checkup and of course the doctor says she was riddled with arthritis and her kidneys was failing and I'm sure he said a whole host of other things but my brain had turned off by then. I was only thinking of our time together, all the walks all the time outside, all the searches for four leaf clovers and hunts for fossils from our youth was coming to an end.

Of course I got the traditional 'take her home and make her as comfortable as possible if you don't want to put her to sleep now.' Put her to sleep? "She's too young for that," I thought. I knew the doctors I worked for were crazy but this is ridiculous I kept telling myself.

I took her home and prepared my mother and sisters for what I knew was inevitable. My mother took it hard because she had been with FiFi just as long as I had and while she was my best friend, she was also hers while I was away at school.

I don't know how I knew but I just knew the day was that day. It wasn't one particular thing. I guess just looking at her eyes and they told me that it was time to let go. Of course no one wanted me to do it. I didn't want to do it, but I knew FiFi did.

I took her to the animal hospital and they let me be alone with her for a moment like we always did for patients and their pets. I thought the divorce was the hardest thing I ever went through until now. I told her how much I loved her and how sorry I was that this was the end. She just looked at me with a forgiving look, at least that's what I thought it was.

I got to hold her paw while she was going to sleep and that's exactly what they do, go to sleep. They're given an injection of a calming tranquilizer before they're given a shot of euthanasia which paralyzes their heart and lungs and the last thing you hear is a big sigh.

My mother found another dog but I never seem to get close to it and over the years she'd had others but I never got close to any of them until I was old enough to get my own dog and that was when I was married.

I'm divorced now and have my own dogs, both of them Pointers. The one has been with my daughter and me less than six months. And the other one has been with us for 6 years and having this information from this book is helpful. Knowing what to expect as Brownie ages helps in the long run.

Rock- Brother, Son, my Dog- Don and Kellie
Rainwater

Rock came into my life by accident. A coworker
asked me to keep him when he was about six
months old. The coworker, who did not have a
place to live, was living out of a tent in the Rocky
Mountains The previous owner said he had Rock
tied up to a tree all day long and the danger of them
being attacked by wild animals or stolen was
immense. I agreed to keep the dog for two or three
weeks until the gentleman found a place to live.
Rock was about six months to a year old by then
and was in training. My roommate had a Labrador
named Abby who was about the same age but with
better training.

Rock and I became attached as we played ball
together and he went through some immense house
training regimens. After the two weeks I learned
that I really love the dog and I didn't want to give it
back to its owner. When he came back to retrieve
Rocky and saw how much Rock was attached to
me, he let me keep him.

Rock became the first rock in my life for over 30
years. I actually had someone to come home to
take care of him. My life of hanging out and just
doing what I wanted to when I wanted to do it came
to an end. He needed food, water, and plenty of
love. This helped me to settle down and to start
college and eventually I settled down completely.

If it wasn't for my Labrador Rock I would have never met my wife Kellie. We met online and we talked back and forth and she really wasn't hooked until she asked me about my dog. A page and a half later, I explained exactly what Rock meant to me. She started dating me and he was coming along too.

She also informed me that if I brought Rock over to her house and her dog did not get along with mine then our relationship was over. We found out that we both had a loving respect and deep affection for all animals and luckily her Pomeranian, Sparky, did not have much trouble with Rock and after a few months we moved in together.

Rock walked my wife down the aisle during our wedding and traveled with us to Florida, Disney World, across the country five times, and he loved every minute of it. We lived five years in the state of Maine and I almost lost Rock one day when he jumped into a river and lost his footing. I had to jump into the river to fish him out. He loved the water and would do anything to go swimming.

We moved to Wyoming from Maine about three years ago. Rock was starting to age and our new house had stairs and he had a hard time climbing up and down. He was a true loyal friend who stood beside my sweet wife and myself until the very end. While I was writing this book, Rock passed away. He was getting close to 14 and evidently was having seizures at night. I came down one morning and his eyes were glazed over, his claws clenched into the carpet, and when I called his name he did not recognize me anymore. I loved the dog more than anything else, but it would be selfish of me to have him go through a few more months or a few more years of pain. I had to let it go.

I've had many dogs in my life but having Rock put to sleep is the hardest decision I ever had to make. Rock was cremated and he sits in his urn at the bottom of the stairs. Every morning my first job was to go to the bottom of the stairs and call him go outside. Now he sits and waits and I talk to him every morning. He is still part of our life. And hopefully I'll see him on the other side a Rainbow Bridge.

About the Authors

Don Rainwater and his wife Kellie live in Wyoming. Don is a teacher in the behavior classroom and the local junior high school. Kellie is a legal student who has ambitions to pursue a legal career at law school. Don and Kellie have six furry children. Murphy a yellow Labrador who is six months old and believes his name is Murphy NO. Rico who is a one year old Chihuahua is Murphy's best friend and confidant. Marley, a York Shire poodle mix, is our old man now. He is 10 years old and was named after Bob Marley the reggae singer. The leader of the pack is Trixie, the spitfire Jack Russell terrier. Trixie runs the show and runs our house. She was also the inspiration for Don and Kellie's first book, "The Jack Russell Terrier: Canine Companion Or Devil Dog." The couple has two cats Pandora, the rescued show cat from the streets of Las Vegas. And Marvann a run-of-the-mill alley cat who was grossly overweight but is full of love.

Gina Stewart lives in Missouri with her two dogs, Brownie – a German shorthaired Pointer and Paige – an English Pointer, and a torturous shell cat named Marble. Her daughter, Madelyne just left to attend the University of Missouri and returns home every chance she gets (to play with the dogs, not visit mom!) Gina has written and published several essays; produced several plays and tons of articles for newspapers and magazines. This is her first book.

2548721

Made in the USA